JUMP STARTS FOR CATECHISTS

Stories that Teach

CARL PFEIFER
AND JANAAN MANTERNACH

Stories that Teach

Twenty-Third Publications
A Division of Bayard
185 Willow Street
P.O. Box 180
Mystic, CT 06355
(860) 536-2611 or (800) 321-0411
www.twentythirdpublications.com
ISBN:1-58595-515-9

Contents

About This Series

The *Jump Starts for Catechists* series offers catechists
quick, hands-on tips for their faith formation sessions.
Each booklet provides practical and "classroom-tested"
information, formation, and ideas
that are valuable for beginning
as well as experienced catechists.
The books are written by some of
Twenty-Third Publications' best-selling authors,
including Gwen Costello, Sr. Mary Kathleen Glavich,
Dan Connors, and Alison Berger.
Other books available in this series include
The Prayer Journey, The Liturgical Year, and *The Early Church.*

Stories that Teach

Story is vitally important in our lives of faith
because it connects with the whole of life.
In this delightful book, the authors provide
ideas and examples for doing just that.
Catechists can learn from the example of Jesus
who used parables to communicate important lessons
about life and faith.
The "modern parables" contained in popular children's stories
are a treasury of imaginative themes, illustrations,
word pictures, and adventure.
Catechists can draw on this treasury for creative
and appealing ways to present faith lessons.

Introduction

Story is one of the most powerful resources
   available to us for teaching religion.
Yet this marvelous tool is too seldom used
   by catechists and religion teachers.
This book is an attempt to change that.
When we speak to religion teachers and catechists
   about the use of story in their classes,
we realize that there is a great deal of interest in
   and enthusiasm for this topic.
But soon, it often seems, both the interest and enthusiasm wane
   and the desire to use story is eclipsed
      by the other "have-to-dos" of teaching.
While many religion textbooks suggest and include stories
   from children's literature in their lesson plans,
some catechists and religion teachers skip over them
   in order to devote more time to what they believe
      is most important.
Story connects with the whole of life.
Children's literature deals with every aspect
   of the human and divine.

It does so unabashedly, perceptively,
    and often in a way that challenges the reader
    to consider a more loving, more careful,
        and wiser way to live.

One Way to Use Story in Class

Most often we use a story
    during the first step of a lesson.
To add to the children's sense
    of how important community can be and is, for example,
    we might read Leo Lionni's *Swimmy* with them.
We simply read it, pause, and go on
    to the next step in the lesson.
Or, we wait for the children to make observations
    or ask questions about the story.
We rarely raise questions about a story,
    nor do we ever tell the children what a story means.
We believe that each child receives a story
    in a unique and personal way.
A good story rarely needs to be explained.
We have found, also, that stories take up residence
    in children's memories.
When they are asked what they remember
    from previous lessons,
    they often will name and retell a story
        while seemingly not being able to recall anything else.

Story Instructs, Empowers, Heals

Besides connecting to the whole of life, story instructs.
G. K. Chesterton, in the chapter titled "The Ethics of Elfland"
    in his book *Orthodoxy*, said that
        the most important things he learned,
        he learned from fairy tales.

A story that reveals
   the power of instruction in literature
      is "Even Teacups Talk" (SS5).
Another value that story has is that it lodges itself
   in the memory and thereby empowers.
This is illustrated in "Telling One's Own Story" (SS).
It tells of how a great rabbi saved his people
      by a certain ritual and prayer.
Years later one of his disciples could no longer
   perform the ritual or remember the prayer.
"All I can do is tell the story," he said to God,
   "and this must be sufficient." And it was.
Story makes us laugh, cry, wonder, imagine. It also heals.
Filling children's minds and hearts with stories
   can affirm the gifts and talents they have
      and also give them hope.
An example of this kind of story is "Let the Music Out" (SS2).
Antonio Stradivari loved music but could not sing.
However, he became the maker of the most famous violins
   in the world.

Jesus Used Story

Perhaps the most important reason for using story
   is that Jesus, and the Hebrew prophets before him,
      taught chiefly through stories.
Whenever Jesus taught or answered a question,
   he told a parable, a story.
His intriguing, challenging stories have continued
   to touch people profoundly for some twenty centuries.
We continue, in the third millennium, to ponder, probe,
   tell, act out, and live by his stories.
He spoke of life's deepest mysteries in stories
   about housewives baking bread and farmers planting seed.

In his stories are taxpayers, unjust judges, rich fools, birds,
   fig trees, servants and masters, the rich and the poor,
   the pious and the sinner, and wise and foolish virgins.
Jesus was one of the best—if not the very best—
   of all teachers who use stories.

Give story a try. To begin, we recommend
   that you build one story per month into your lesson plan.
That would amount to nine stories a year.
In the chapters that follow, we will choose a theme
   and suggest stories that fit into that theme.

Key to abbreviations used in the text:

SS   *Sower's Seeds*

SS2   *More Sower's Seeds: Second Planting*

SS3   *Fresh Packet of Sower's Seeds: Third Planting*

SS4   *Sower's Seeds Aplenty: Fourth Planting*

SS5   *Sower's Seeds of Encouragement: Fifth Planting*

SS6   *Sower's Seeds that Nurture Family Values: Sixth Planting*

All of these books are edited by Brian Cavanaugh and available
from Paulist Press, Mahwah, N.J.

CHAPTER ONE

Christian Community

Community is a characteristic that has to be experienced
   before it is valued.
It has to be witnessed before it is desired.
We know this is true because we have experienced
   community again and again in our families,
      our parish, our neighborhood, and in schools.
What is profoundly true of community is that we need it
   because it embraces, supports, inspires, and challenges us all.
It provides an environment in which people survive
   and thrive together, and in which a belief system
      and a faith tradition can take root and grow.

Creating Community in Religion Classes

During the years that Anna Thompson was coordinator
   of religious education at Holy Trinity Parish
      in Washington, DC,
   Carl and I were catechists in the parish program.
Anna was genuinely interested in what we taught
   in our classes, but her main concern was
      that we create community with the young people in our classes.

She encouraged eating a snack and talking together
before we began any actual instruction.
She told us again and again
that the children were to see Christ in us,
but we were also to see Christ in the children.
One of our first tasks was to learn the names of the children,
and during subsequent classes to employ creative ways
for getting to know each one.
Respect and reverence for ourselves and each one of them
were to be hallmarks of our endeavors.
All these practices worked, and lasting friendships
grew out of those years.
A story that describes some of what happened to all of us
during that time as we committed ourselves
to seeing the divine in each other, is "The Rabbi's Gift" (SS).
An abbot went to ask advice of his friend, a rabbi.
The monastery the abbot was head of
was going through difficult times.
The rabbi gave the abbot a message:
"The messiah is among you."
When the abbot repeated this message to his monks,
they wondered what it could mean.
Little by little they began to treat one another
with a special respect and reverence.
Before long the monastery was again filled with prayer and hope,
and people came from long distances for spiritual counsel.

Creating Community through Partnership

The partnership aspect is another essential element
in the creation of community.
What flows from or is produced by the work that we do,
in partnership with each other,
continues the reign of God here on earth.

Being a partner with someone helps build friendships
  as well as continue God's work on earth.
We learned the truth of this by giving children
  opportunities to work in pairs.
Two of the girls who had been partners asked
  if they might work together again.
They told us that they hadn't known each other before
  and were becoming friends.
Kindness is at the heart of community.
It is something that everyone needs.
It can change the direction of a person's life
  and add immeasurably to the lives of many others.
The power of kindness is revealed in the story,
  "Remember Those Who Help" (SS5).

Community Creates an Environment

Community is a primary goal in everything that we do
  in our religion classes and catechetical settings
  because it creates an environment
    for relationships to grow.
It also provides children and young people
  with the experience of building friendships
    and maintaining them.
Within a loving community,
  children can learn how to listen well
  and experience the joy of being listened to.
They can attain the self-esteem that comes
  from the divine being recognized and affirmed in them
  as well as from their own recognition and affirmation
    of the divine in others.
The children can learn how comforting it is
  to be helped by others,
  and of the need to be willing to reach out to others.

Within a community of faith, children and young people can learn
    that they are not only witnesses of Jesus,
        but that they are the presence of Jesus in the world.
Children's literature is one of our greatest resources
    for helping children and young people capture the meaning
    and experience of community.
The following are some of the best books we know of
    on the topic, along with suggested age levels.
The Glassmakers of Gurven, by Marlys Boddy, is a story
    about a small town of people building themselves a church.
A crisis occurs when the glassmakers can't agree
    on the color of glass that should go in the big window.
How the glassmakers resolve their disagreement
    creates a delightful and wonderful story of community.
This is a good book to use with third graders,
    especially if they are learning what it means to be "church."
Little Blue and Little Yellow, by Leo Lionni, is about two spots
    who are best friends.
Their friendship unites them in a surprising and mysterious way.
When children hear this story, they understand more
    about being united with Jesus in the Eucharist.
We recommend this story for parents and catechists of children
    preparing for First Communion.
Swimmy, another book by Lionni, is also
    a powerful story of community.
Yo! Yes? by Chris Raschka, is a picture book
    about an African-American boy who calls, "Yo!"
    to a shy and friendless Caucasian boy,
        and offers him friendship.
Their acceptance of each other is celebrated with a high five
    and the single word, "Yow."
This story can be used in any lesson in which there is reflection
    and sharing on the theme of friendship.

CHAPTER TWO

Seeing Others as Equal

There is an expectancy, and rightfully so,
    that we who are Catholic Christians treat one another
        with respect;
that nothing—race, color, class, creed, sex and sexual orientation,
    disability, clothes, education, poverty, or wealth—
        should make a difference.
Children capture the truth of that expectancy
    when they are exposed to stories in which people genuinely
    and actively care about others no matter what they look like,
        no matter what their circumstances.
A good example is "The Beggar King" (SS2).
The story tells of a young man who gives all he has to a beggar
    and discovers he has given it to his king.
The king makes the generous and loving young man his successor.

Racism

Racism is one of the greatest evils in our society
    and is a pernicious affront to the truth

that everyone is worthy of respect,
and everyone is of equal worth.
Story is a great resource for helping children see
the horror of racism
and appreciate behavior that is color-blind.
A wonderful story about the power of generous,
accepting behavior is "A Simple Gesture."
It's an anecdote from the life of Jackie Robinson,
the first black player in the major leagues (SS3).

Children's Literature and Prejudice

There are many other stories and poems
about prejudice and the damage it inflicts
as well as about heroism in dealing with prejudice.
In *Amazing Grace*, by Mary Hoffman, schoolmates tell Grace
that because she's a girl and black she can't be Peter Pan
in an upcoming play.
But after her mother and grandmother
lovingly reaffirm all possibilities,
Grace tries out and plays the role to universal acclaim.
The Story of Ruby Bridges, by Robert Coles,
tells how a child braves hatred and prejudice
prayerfully and courageously.
In *Be Good to Eddie Lee*, by Virginia Fleming, two children
don't want to include another child who is disabled.
They finally accept him and learn an important lesson.
Mrs. Katz and Tush, by Patricia Polacco, is a warm and loving story
of an unusual friendship between an African-American boy
and an elderly Jewish neighbor.
In *The Witch of Blackbeard Pond*, by Elizabeth George Speare,
Kit, a young and lonely woman, becomes friends
with a lone and mysterious figure
known as the Witch of Blackbeard Pond.

With her she feels free and at peace.
But when their friendship is discovered, Kit is faced with suspicion,
    fear, anger, and a witch trial.
This story won the John Newbery Medal.
People, by Peter Spier, is a wonderful book
    that helps children appreciate people of different racial,
        socioeconomic, and cultural backgrounds.
In *The Cay*, by Theodore Taylor, Philip has looked down
    on black-skinned people all his life.
Suddenly, he's a refugee from a fatal shipwreck and dependent
    on an extraordinary West Indian man named Timothy.
The story connects us with their struggle for survival,
    as well as with the boy's efforts to adjust to blindness
    and to understand the dignified, wise, and loving man
        who is his companion.
Let the Celebrations Begin, by Margaret Wild and Julie Vivas,
    tells about the concentration camp Belsen.
Miriam and other women plan a very special party for the children.
They make incredible toys out of scraps of material,
    rags, torn pockets, buttons—anything.
Finally, as World War II ends, the great celebration,
    which they planned and worked for, begins.

What about our own prejudices? Do we always behave
    as though everyone is deserving of respect?
Perhaps what all of us need is a pair of granny's glasses
    ("Granny's Glasses," by Walter Buchanan, SS4).
Granny can see the good in a person
    when everyone else sees the bad side.

CHAPTER THREE

Treating Others with Compassion

Our world is in great need of the qualities
  contained in the principle "Do no harm."
Compassion and justice must be fostered, modeled,
  inspired, taught, and expected of everyone.
Children can indeed learn how to be compassionate and just;
  we can teach them what it looks and feels like.
Our godchildren's father repeatedly tells Angela and Miguel:
  "We have no right to hurt anyone."
Jesus speaks of compassion in his well-known parable
  of the Good Samaritan (Luke 10:29–37).
  A man fell victim to robbers as he went down from Jerusalem
  to Jericho. They stripped and beat him and went off leaving
  him half-dead.

  A priest happened to be going down that road, but when he
  saw him, he passed by on the opposite side. Likewise, a Levite
  came to the place, and when he saw him, he passed by on the
  opposite side.

  But a Samaritan traveler who came upon him was moved

with compassion at the sight. He approached the victim, poured oil and wine over his wounds and bandaged them. Then he lifted him up on his own animal, took him to an inn, and cared for him.

The next day he took out two silver coins and gave them to the innkeeper with the instruction, "Take care of him. If you spend more than I have given you, I will pay you on my way back."

After Jesus finished his story, he asked: "Which of these three, in your opinion, was neighbor to the robbers' victim?" A man answered, "The one who treated him with mercy." Then Jesus said to him (and to us), "Go and do likewise."

Models of Compassion and Justice

People who lived extraordinary lives of compassion and justice
   are also great models.
Their stories are found in books about saints
   and other holy people.
We recommend *Butler's Lives of the Saints.*
The books are arranged according to the months of the year
   as well as by the feastday of each saint.
The life of each saint is told in detail.
When we use these books, we choose the parts of a saint's life
   that we want to emphasize.
Other models of compassion are the young people
   whose service-oriented and creative actions
      make the world a better place.
In 1999, a youth conference in St. Louis drew 23,000 people.
One of the young people who addressed the session
   was sixteen-year-old Craig Kielburger,
      founder of Free the Children, an international organization
         working to free children from poverty and exploitation.

The Toronto teen said everyone must share
   the gifts given by God to make the world a better place.
He urged youths to live their faith through action.
"When we carry the message and rally more people," he said,
   "that's how we're going to change this world."

Stories of Compassion

Some of the stories we've used in religion classes,
   including Bible stories about Jesus showing compassion,
      are listed below.
The Bible. "The Feeding of the Five Thousand,"
   found in Matthew 14:13–21, Mark 6:34–44, and Luke 9:10–17;
   "The Good Samaritan," Luke 10:29–37;
   "Blind Bartimaeus," Mark 10:46–52 and Luke 18:35–43.
The Book of Virtues, by William J. Bennett.
   "Old Mr. Rabbit's Thanksgiving Dinner," by Carolyn Bailey;
   "The Legend of the Dipper," retold by J. Berg Esenwein
      and Marietta Stockard;
   "Grandmother's Table," adapted from the Brothers Grimm.
The Book of Virtues for Young People, by William J. Bennett.
   "If I Can Stop One Heart from Breaking," by Emily Dickinson;
   "The Angel of the Battlefield," by Joanna Strong
      and Tom B. Leonard.
Stone Soup, by Marcia Brown.
The Paper Crane, by Molly Bang.
Shibumi and the Kitemaker, by Mercer Mayer.
An Angel for Solomon Singer, by Cynthia Rylant.
Tico and the Golden Wings, by Leo Lionni.
With Love at Christmas, by Mem Fox.
Saint Valentine, by Robert Sabuda.
The Story of Jumping Mouse, by John Steptoe.
Knots on a Counting Rope, by Martin and John Archambault.

An exquisite story in which the "hero" feeds the needs
   and hungers of the spirit and which we consider
   a classic compassion story is *The Dancing Man*, by Marlys Boddy.
Joseph, an orphan, lives in a poor village by the Baltic Sea.
He realizes, while he is still young, that life in the village
   is dreary and hard,
      but he sees that all around him the world dances.
Then one evening a mysterious stranger appears on the shore.
He says to Joseph, "I'm the Dancing Man and I have a gift for you."
The old man dances down the shore and Joseph follows.
A sharp gust of wind blows and suddenly the man is gone.
But in the sand lay his silver shoes,
   and Joseph knows they are meant for him.
When Joseph grows up, he puts on the shoes
   and dances from village to village, taking away
      some of the dreariness and bringing happiness to the people.
Joseph later passes on to another child
   what had been passed on to him.

In preparing a session, determine where you feel
   one of the stories suggested above, or another story like these,
      will fit into a class.
We usually read a story like this after the story from the Bible
   has been listened to and talked and prayed about.
Give your children plenty of opportunities to express in words
   and drawings how the principle "Do no harm"
      might be lived out in their daily lives.

CHAPTER FOUR

Making Moral Choices

In the last chapter we quoted a Buddhist principle:
"Do no harm." In part, that suggests a moral stance.
If we are intentional about not hurting others,
 we are acting as Jesus acted in his life and living out the call
  of our baptism—to be his disciples.
In helping children grasp what it means to do no harm
 and to live as disciples of Jesus,
it is good to consider this question with them:
 "What does love look like?"
One way to describe what love looks like
 is a change of heart, a conversion.
Denise, a sixth-grader in one of our religion classes,
 describes this kind of conversion as she experienced it.
Her mother and dad said that Denise and her brother Eric
 should start doing more jobs around the house.
Her mother wasn't able to do all the small jobs by herself.
Denise replied that she had a lot of homework,
 and went off to do it.

While she was doing her homework, Denise thought
  about what her mother had said.
She had a change of heart and decided
  to help her mother more often.

Honesty and Truthfulness

Another answer to the question, "What does love look like?"
  is telling the truth, no matter how tempted
    one might be to lie.
A fable that shows us what this looks like
  is "The Honest Woodsman"
    (*The Children's Book of Virtues*, William J. Bennett).
A poor woodcutter loses his axe in the river one day.
A water fairy appears, shows the woodsman an axe of silver,
  and asks if it belongs to him.
The honest woodsman tells the fairy that no,
  the silver axe was not his.
The same happens as the water fairy next appears
  with a golden axe.
Finally, the fairy brings the lost axe up from the river bottom,
  and the woodsman says that yes,
    this is indeed his old axe.
Then the fairy gives the woodsman his axe,
  along with the axes of gold and silver,
    as a reward for his honesty.
"Honest Abe," a story in *The Children's Book of Heroes*,
  by William J. Bennett, also demonstrates integrity.
Abraham Lincoln walked three miles to return
  the six cents he had overcharged a customer.
Our favorite children's story about honesty is
  The Empty Pot, by Demi.
All the children in the kingdom receive a flower seed
  from the Emperor with this instruction:

"Whoever can show me their best in a year's time
    will succeed me to the throne."
Ping does everything to get his seed to bloom but it doesn't.
At the end of the year he has to face the Emperor
    with an empty pot without a flower.
Other children come with beautiful and unusual flowers.
Ping feels humiliated and sad until the reason for the seed's
    lack of power to grow is announced by the Emperor.
Ping's honesty and integrity is revealed at that moment.
He is rewarded, not only with the Emperor's great admiration,
    but also with being named as his successor.

To Love Well Is a Choice

All of us, including our children and young people,
    are aware that the sum total of our moral life
        depends upon the choices we make.
Along with the question "What does love look like?"
    we also need to ask, "How do our actions reveal
        God's action in us?"
Many stories in children's literature illustrate characters
    who respond or fail to respond to the call
        to do the loving thing.
The Braids Girl, by Lisa McCourt, is a special story about Izzy,
    a girl who goes with her grandfather to a home
        called the "Family Togetherness Home."
Another girl is living at the home with her mother.
Izzy tries to help the girl by giving her things,
    but gradually learns that "things" are not what she needs most.
With a little help from her grandfather, Izzy finally realizes
    that the girl longs for and needs a friend.
When Izzy offers the girl her friendship, everything changes.
In Shoemaker Martin, by Leo Tolstoy, a shoemaker waits all day
    for a promised visit from Jesus.

While he's waiting, he welcomes two visitors into his home
   and offers each of them food, drink, a warm coat, and money.
He also lovingly negotiates peace and good will
   between a market woman and a poor boy who had stolen
      one of her apples.
Later, when he takes his Bible down to read again the passage
   he has pondered all day, he learns that Jesus had visited him
      in the people he had helped.

Stories inspire. Memories of heroic actions can linger
   in children's imaginations
      and become the bedrock of their moral lives.
That is a primary reason for stocking their imaginations
   with stories.
Here are four ways to bring story into effective play
   in catechetical and religious education settings.
1. Provide children with several issues of the local newspapers.
Invite them to find stories that show people acting morally,
   people doing something in a loving manner.
2. Give the children many opportunities to write and tell,
   sketch or draw their own stories, to reveal how they
   or someone else acted generously, honestly, lovingly,
      unselfishly, or responsibly—or who did the opposite.
3. Connect stories from children's literature, from the newspapers,
   and the children's own stories with stories in the Bible
      that are about Jesus doing the loving thing.
4. Use poetry. We usually read a poem aloud twice.
Then after a silent pause, we invite anyone in the class
   who wishes to do so, to tell how they feel
      about the poem's story.
Further activity might involve a discussion.

CHAPTER FIVE

Forgiveness and Reconciliation

God is present and active in our efforts to forgive
and to reconcile.
When we forgive and reconcile, we're responding
to the promptings of God's grace and mercy.
God's life is at work in us.
Helping children recognize the value of forgiving
and reconciling, and inspiring them to be
forgiving and reconciling, is at the heart of what we do
as catechists and religion teachers.
Yet teaching the art of forgiveness and reconciliation is hard.
Experiences of reconciliation and forgiveness happen
in relationships, primarily between two parties,
and the causes of the rift or breakdown are often
completely or partially hidden.
Nevertheless, it is vital to overcome the hardships
because a community's life and spirit suffer
when some of its members do not forgive and reconcile.

Stories about Forgiveness

Most of us, including our children and young people,
    find stories of forgiveness and reconciliation
        inspiring and instructive.
Such stories can be catalysts for searching out the stories
    of forgiveness and reconciliation that have occurred
        in our own lives.
They can also increase our awareness of the importance
    of helping young people be forgiving and reconciling.
There are many stories of this type in children's literature.
In *The Legend of the Persian Carpet*, by Tomie de Paola,
    a precious diamond, loved by a king and his people,
        is stolen from the palace.
When the sun reflected through the diamond,
    the rooms were filled with a million rainbows.
Without the diamond, they were filled with shadows and gloom.
The king is devastated until a young boy finds a way to bring
    the colors back to the room
    and the king back to his people.
This is a story of turning from darkness to light,
    healing and restoration.
Even If I Did Something Awful? by Barbara Shook Hazen,
    is about a child who has broken
        one of her mother's treasures.
To make sure of her mother's forgiveness
    and unconditional love, she keeps identifying
    different scenarios and repeating the question,
        "Even if I did something awful?"
In *A Bargain for Frances*, by Russell Hoban,
    Frances and Thelma are friends, but Frances frequently gets
        the bad end of a deal when she plays with Thelma.
When Frances goes to Thelma's to play tea party
    and make mud cakes, her mother warns Frances to be careful.

Frances finds out she's been taken but cleverly figures out
    a way to right the wrong and save the friendship.
This story not only deals with breaking faith in a relationship.
It also reveals how important reconciliation is
    to maintain friendships.
And to Think that We Thought that We'd Never Be Friends,
    by Mary Ann Hoberman, is a story of "making up,"
        which is the activity of reconciling.
This story also shows the power that "making up" has
    to create harmony and community.
In *The Rag Coat*, by Lauren Mills, Minna's father is dead,
    her family is poor, and she doesn't have a coat to wear.
A group of mothers who quilt together decide
    to make Minna a coat from scraps of old clothing.
When Minna goes to school in the rag coat,
    the other children make fun of her.
Saddened by their behavior Minna goes to the woods.
She remembers some words of her father, and cries.
Minna then returns to school and shares the stories
    of the rags in her coat.
Acceptance and forgiveness take place.
The Crystal Heart: A Vietnamese Legend, by Aaron Shepard,
    tells of Mi Nuong, the daughter of a great mandarin,
        who hears a song that floats to her from a distance.
She waits by her window hoping to hear the singer again.
When she doesn't, she becomes ill.
To help her get well the great mandarin sends a messenger
    to locate the person who sang the song.
However, when Mi Nuong sees that the singer
    is a common fisherman, she laughs at her folly.
The fisherman is deeply hurt, grows ill, and dies.
His body is found by the villagers,
    who notice that there is a large crystal heart on his chest.

The crystal heart washes ashore by the mandarin's palace
    where it is made into a tea cup for his daughter.
When she goes to sip tea from it the face of the fisherman
    is on the surface of the tea and his sweet song fills the room.
Mi Nuong's eyes fill with tears of sorrow.
One drops into the cup, releasing the spirit of the fisherman.
Mi Nuong later marries, but she still often hears
    the song of the fisherman echo softly in her heart.

Using These Stories in Class

One way we have successfully used stories of forgiveness
    is to dramatically read or tell them.
We then invite two or three volunteers to retell the story
    using their own words.
Others in the group are given an opportunity to fill in
    what was left out in the retelling
    or to indicate parts in the retelling
      that were not in the original.
Another interesting and meaningful activity
     is to put the children in pairs or small groups,
      then tell them to change the ending of the story
      and give reasons for the change.
Questions that you may want to ask of a story are:
How do you feel about what happened in the story?
What do you think you will always remember about this story?
What other stories have you heard that are like this one?
Sometimes we pause after a story to give everyone
    an opportunity to silently think of things we have done
      that we might regret,
    as well as of things we need to forgive.
Then, still in silence, we plan how we will forgive
    both ourselves and others.

CHAPTER SIX

God's Presence

Presence is an extraordinary concept
  in the Catholic Christian tradition.
Its meaning is connected with the presence of Christ
    in the assembly that gathers for Mass, the priest presider,
      the Scripture readings, and the bread and wine.
His eucharistic presence celebrates and reminds us
    of his presence with us at every moment
      through people and all creation.
The poem "Remember," by Christy Kenneally,
    found in his book *Miracles and Me*, describes Jesus
      speaking to his disciples at the Last Supper.
In this poem, Jesus asks the disciples to remember
    the many ways he had been with them.
He tells them he will continue to be with them
    in the bread and wine they share when they gather
      as a community to pray.

God Is Present in All Creation

We also believe in the presence of God in all creation
  which includes the human family.

When we talk about God's presence, we say things like,
   "God's life is in us" or "God dwells in our hearts,"
       or we use the word "soul" to identify God's indwelling.
To awaken children to God's presence and to continually deepen
   their sense of the presence of the divine in them
       is to transform their lives and equip them to live
           faithfully, lovingly, joyfully, and with hope.
One way we can capture children's imaginations
   about God's presence is to provide them with meaningful
   and creative answers to the question,
       "What is God like?"
One example is found in the book *The Runaway Bunny*,
   by Margaret Wise Brown.
This story is about a little bunny who wants to run away.
His mother's response is,
   "If you run away I will run after you.
   for you are my little bunny."
The bunny describes a number of ways
   that will make it possible for him to get away.
His mother lovingly counters each one by telling him
   how she will find him.
Like the mother in the story, God promises
   to be with us always, wherever we go.
God's presence creates a relationship that comforts
   and strengthens.

Presence Is a Giving of Self

Another story that reveals God's gift of presence
   is "The King's Great Gift" (SS3).
A wise king who cared for his people disguised himself
   as a poor man and went to the public baths.
While there he visited the man in the basement
   who kept the water heated.

The two became good friends.
When the king finally revealed his identity, the man was moved.
"You gave me the gift of yourself," he said.
Wind and air, one and the same atmospheric reality,
    are often connected to God's mysterious presence.
They help us believe in a God we can't see
    because the wind and air can't be seen either.
They are vital to our existence, which is also true of God's presence
    in our lives and in the whole of creation.
A poem that deals with the wind's unseen presence
    in a near mystical way is "Who Has Seen the Wind?"
        by Christina Rossetti.
Who has seen the wind?
Neither I nor you;
But when the leaves hang trembling,
The wind is passing through.

Other Children's Literature Selections

In *The Collector of Moments,* by Quint Buchholz,
    a solitary boy is befriended by Max, an artist.
The boy spends days in Max's studio, and each evening
    at dusk he plays his violin.
Sometimes the artist sings along;
    sometimes he's just silent.
When the artist goes on a journey, he leaves behind
    a surprise exhibition for the boy.
The boy studies each of the pictures and discovers
    answers to all his questions.
Through his relationship with the artist the boy
    accepts his own gift, which he eventually uses
        to inspire and teach others.
Shalinar's Song, by Daniel J. Porter, tells about the son
    of the Master Builder of the Kingdom.

When Shalinar is six, he surprises his father with the song
    his hammer makes as it hits the chisel on its mark.
His father tells him, "The song of God is in your heart, Shalinar.
    It rings through the work you do.
Always think of God as you work and your labor will shine."
After his father dies, Shalinar becomes the Master Builder.
He surpasses his father's skill in the buildings he creates,
    but he fails or refuses to listen to the song of God in his heart.
As he grows older, he feels lonely and empty until one day
    when he hears beautiful music played by a small boy.
The music brings Shalinar back to his father's words,
    "The song of God is in your heart, Shalinar."
Shalinar eventually recovers that song.
In the story *In God's Name*, by Sandy Eisenberg Sasso,
    all the people of the world set out to find God's name.
Each one, in turn, names God according to
    what he or she feels and believes God is like.
They all believe their name for God is the right one.
Then they look into a lake that is clear and quiet like a mirror,
    God's mirror, and see their own faces
        and the faces of all the others.
In so doing they realize that all the names for God are good
    and no name is better than another.
In the end their voices come together,
        and they call God One.

Our loving and caring presence in children's lives can help them
    believe in the presence of a loving and caring God,
        someone who is always with them and for them.
God will never abandon them,
    but will pursue them like Thompson's "Hound of Heaven"
        or like the mother in *The Runaway Bunny*.

CHAPTER SEVEN

Advent

Advent is a four-week season that begins on the Sunday
    closest to November 30 and ends on Christmas Day.
It is a time of joyful expectation as we wait for Christ
    to come into our lives.
Expectation and waiting are symbolized in the Advent wreath.
The base of the wreath is usually made of fresh evergreens
    that encircle three purple candles and a pink one.
On the first Sunday of Advent, one of the purple candles is lit
    and a special prayer is said.
On the second Sunday, a second purple candle is lit
    along with the first one, and another prayer is said.
The pink candle is lit on the third Sunday,
    traditionally called Gaudete Sunday.
It expresses a joyful note of anticipation within the season.
The lighting of all four candles on the Sunday before Christmas
    heralds the final moments of waiting.
Part of the challenge of Advent is to find ways
    to involve the children's religious imaginations
        in understanding expectancy and waiting.

One of the more successful things we've done is invite
   mothers and fathers who are expecting a baby to visit our class.
The parents come prepared to share their stories.
They may tell the children how long they've been waiting
   for this child, or what they plan to do as a couple or family
      to welcome the child.
Then we read aloud *Everett Anderson's Nine Months Long*,
   by Lucille Clifton, or *The Baby Sister*, by Tomie de Paola.
We give the children opportunities to remember
   and tell stories about their own experiences of waiting.
We also reflect together on how hard it is sometimes to wait,
   but also how waiting can help us grow up.

Unselfish Giving and Action in Advent

Advent reflects the longing for the birth of Jesus
   that occurred centuries ago.
Advent also guides us to look for Christ's "second coming"
   at the end of the world.
But Advent's most immediate longing is for
   the coming of the risen Christ in our own lives.
One of the most important things we can do with children
   during Advent is to develop their capacity
      for generosity and unselfish behavior.
We can do this by helping them make the connection
   between the coming of Christ into the world
      and their own presence in the world as his followers.
Involving the children in practical, hands-on activities
   is a good way to reinforce this connection.
Stocking children's imaginations with stories of generosity
   is a tried and true way of initiating them into the spirit
      of preparation that is the mark of the Advent season.
The story "The Face in the Window," (SS) might be read
   to children at the beginning of Advent.

You can use it for ideas of things they can do together
    to help the poor in your neighborhood and community.
Do not be afraid to challenge and encourage children
    to embody a selfless and generous spirit.
Another story that fascinates children is, "The Christmas Shell,"
    adapted by Gerald Horton Bath (SS4).
This story gently suggests that what we put into a gift
    is part of its value, part of the sacrifice.

Advent Stories in Children's Literature

The meaning of Advent can be found in many pieces
    of children's literature.
In *Everett Anderson's Christmas Coming*, by Lucille Clifton,
    Everett becomes more excited
    as each of the five days before Christmas goes by.
In joyful text and glorious, colorful drawings the story
    of Everett's wait and the coming of Christmas is poignantly told.
In *Maria*, by Theodore Taylor, an eleven-year-old longs
    to have a float in the town's Christmas parade.
How the Gonzagas solve their problem in time
    provides a moving conclusion to one girl's struggle
      to break through cultural and economic barriers.
Her story emphasizes the true spirit of Christmas.
The Christmas Miracle of Jonathan Toomey, by Susan Wojciechowski,
    is a unique story about preparing for Christmas.
A small boy and his widowed mother gently warm
    the sad heart of a woodcarver as he carves
      a Christmas crèche for them.
The biblical stories behind the Jesse Tree,
    as well as how to make one, are told
      in *Advent Stories and Activities* by Anne E. Neuberger.

CHAPTER EIGHT

Christmas

Christmas captures the imaginations of children and adults
    more than any other holy day or holiday.
This feastday, the solemnity of the Incarnation, is
    second in liturgical importance only to
        the annual celebration of Easter.
At Christmas, a feeling of expectancy fills the air
    and merry greetings abound.
Long before the day arrives, lighted trees shine on lawns,
    in town squares, stores, businesses, and homes.
"Giving trees" sprout up near side entrances of churches.
Besides adding to the beauty of the season,
    the Christmas tree is an important and much loved symbol.
Choosing a tree and decorating it
    often involves the whole family.
Fir, spruce, and pine are the most popular Christmas trees.
However, millions of American families today decorate
    fireproof artificial trees.
Many others buy living trees and plant them in their yard
    or garden after Christmas, or give them to a park.

In spite of the tree's dominant role at Christmastime,
    many children don't know any of the history or the legends
    connected to the Christmas tree.
They are often surprised to discover
    that the first Christmas trees
    were not decorated as they are now.
Three delightful stories about Christmas trees are found
    in *The Catholic Source Book*, by Peter Klein.
You can also find information about the tradition
    of the Christmas tree, as well as other Christmas traditions,
    in *Catholic Customs & Traditions*, by Greg Dues,
    and *Advent & Lent Activities for Children*,
        by Shiela Kielly and Sheila Geraghty.

The Christmas Crèche

The crèche is another Christmas symbol much loved
    by children and adults.
Another name for the crèche is a Nativity set.
A crèche or Nativity set contains figures of Mary, Joseph,
    the Christ Child, shepherds, sheep, and barn animals.
The Christ Child is usually wrapped in "swaddling" clothes
    and is lying on a bed of straw.
The Three Kings are added on the feast of the Epiphany.
You'll often find a crèche or Nativity set
    beneath Christmas trees in homes and churches.
The custom of using a Christmas crèche derives from a practice
    begun by St. Francis of Assisi around the year 1223.
St. Francis celebrated Christmas Mass in a barn or cave
    with animals and straw.

The Nativity Story

Most children never tire of the story of the first Christmas,
   whether from the Bible or from children's literature.
Again, as with stories of trees, there are many, many versions
   of the story of Jesus' birth.
They are often set within particular cultures
   in which customs dictate the telling of the story.
The setting for *The Night of Las Posadas*, by Tomie de Paola,
   is Santa Fe, New Mexico, where Christmas Eve is celebrated
      with the traditional procession called "Las Posadas."
A beautiful book written in both Spanish and English,
   created by Charito Calvachi Wakefield,
      is *Navidad Latinoamericana/Latin American Christmas*.
It contains Christmas traditions, hymns, prayers, and practices
   from twenty-five Latin American countries.

Christmas Stories in Children's Literature

Children's lives will be enriched if their minds and hearts
   are filled with the legends and stories of Christmas.
In *The Best Gift for Mom*, by Lee Klein, Jonathan's father is dead.
One evening after Jonathan has lied about his father's death,
   his mom tells him about how his father died.
Jonathan remembers how his father used to put him to sleep
   when he was little.
Using that memory, he gives his mom a special Christmas gift.
The story *Jacob's Gift*, by Max Lucado, tells about
   a carpenter's apprentice in Rabbi Simeon's shop.
The Rabbi announces to the boys that whoever builds
   the best project will work with him on the new synagogue.
Jacob thinks long and hard about what he will build
   and finally decides to make a new kind of animal feed trough.
It is the best work he has ever done.

But that night he becomes aware that there's a new baby
  in the stable near his father's inn,
    without a place to sleep.
How and why Jacob is selected to help the rabbi
  even though he has given away his "work"
    makes for an unusually beautiful Christmas tale.
The Gift of the Magi, by O. Henry, is a classic story
  of a young couple who are very poor.
It's Christmas Eve and each wants to give the other
  a longed-for present.
How they manage to buy the gifts is a story
  of amazing sacrifice and deep love.
*Christmas Gif': An Anthology of Christmas Poems, Songs,
  and Stories Written By and About African Americans,*
    compiled by Charlamae Hill Rollins.
This collection includes wonderful Christmas poems,
  several by Charlamae's friend, Langston Hughes.
A Christmas Story, by Brian Wildsmith, is an original
  and enchanting presentation of the Nativity.
Wildsmith's rich paintings
  with their brilliant colors and shining gold,
    reflect the miracle of the Christ Child's birth
      and joyously celebrate its beauty.
In *The Best Gift of All,* by Cornelia Wilkeshuis,
  Prince Irenus, the young son of King Balthasar,
    decides to follow the star so he can also see the new Prince.
Irenus takes along his red bouncing ball,
  his favorite book, and even his beloved dog Pluton, as gifts.
On the way he finds others who need his gifts more,
  so when he arrives at the stable, he has nothing left
    to give the Prince of Peace.
The Best Gift of All is a wonderful story for children to act out.

CHAPTER NINE

Lent

Many Catholics have vivid memories of the strict practices
    that once marked the season of Lent.
There was a penitential aura about the season.
We could feel Lent in our bones.
This feeling still lingers
    and continues to color Lent for us.
The Ash Wednesday ritual of applying blessed ashes
    on our foreheads was significant.
The formula prayed while the ashes were applied
    was a grim reminder of who we essentially are:
       "Remember that you are dust
       and unto dust you shall return."
Ash Wednesday remains the significant introduction to Lent.
While the above formula is still in use,
    the one more frequently prayed today is,
       "Turn from sin and live the gospel."

Fasting

To turn from sin is to turn toward what is good,
    toward a more loving way of being in the world.

Lent, therefore, is an ideal time to provide children
  with the kind of nurture that increases in them
    an attachment to goodness.
Story is a unique source of that kind of nurture.
One that does this both powerfully and gently is
  Dan Clark's story "Puppies for Sale"
    (*Chicken Soup for the Soul*, Jack Canfield).
A little boy wants to buy a puppy.
When he sees one that is limping, he tells the owner
  that is the puppy he wants to buy.
The owner tries to talk the boy out of it, saying that
  the puppy will never run and jump like the others.
At that the boy shows the man his crippled leg.
"The puppy will need someone who understands," he says.
Another story frequently read at soup suppers during Lent
  is *Stone Soup*, by Marcia Brown.
It deals creatively and provocatively with turning from sin
  toward what is good,
    a more loving way of being in the world.
In *Shiloh*, by Phyllis Reynolds Naylor, a boy's willingness
  to do anything to save an abused dog from a cruel owner
    is a powerful story of goodness in a child.
This story won the John Newbery Medal.
The Hundred Penny Box, by Sharon Bell Mathis,
  tells of a small child poignantly sensitive
    to what an elderly relative needs.
He does what he has to do
  to make sure it is not taken from her.
In *The Jade Stone*, by Caryn Yacowitz,
  Chan Lo disobeys the Great Emperor of all China,
    in spite of his fear of punishment,
      because he can't go against what he knows he has to do.

In the story *The Quiltmaker's Gift*, by Jeff Brumbeau,
   a generous quiltmaker with magic in her fingers
      sews the most beautiful quilts in the world.
How she changes a greedy king who yearns for one of her quilts
   is at the heart of this story.

Prayer

Another basic lenten practice is prayer.
Some of the prayers that are part of Lent arise from
   the colors, the symbols, the food, the music, and the rituals.
Helping children experience these elements
   puts them in touch with Lent's spirit and meaning.
Several years ago we were catechists to fifth
   and sixth grade children.
On the first Sunday of Lent we covered the table
   with a purple cloth and placed on it a large crucifix
      and a bowl of pretzels.
We invited the children to talk about each item.
The children didn't know the pretzel legend,
   so we told them this story.
According to the legend,
   monks formed dough into shapes
   that resembled arms folded in prayer.
They baked the pretzels, then gave them out to children
   as a reward for learning their prayers.
During Lent we always like to pray the Way of the Cross
   with the children we teach.
A booklet we have used again and again as a guide is
   Praying the Stations with Children, by Gwen Costello.
We have also had the children write their own version
   of each of the stations and have used these versions
      to walk the Way of the Cross.

Almsgiving

Almsgiving is another lenten discipline.
Essentially it means reaching out to the poor,
    the sick, and the needy.
Children are easily inspired to this practice,
    through opportunities to do it with others,
    through the example of adults,
      and through stories in which the characters
        act compassionately and generously.
One such story is "Heroes," which tells about
    the touching encounter between Babe Ruth
      and a small boy (SS).
Another moving story is "The Visit," by Debbie Herman,
    found in *Chicken Soup for the Kid's Soul.*

More Stories of Caring People

Stories about saints and other people who cared and care,
    in a radical way, for the poor, the sick, and the dying
    provide models and inspiration for living out
      generosity towards others.
All Saints, by Robert Ellsberg, is an excellent resource
    for stories of "saints, prophets, and witnesses for our time."
The book includes Dorothy Day, Mother Teresa of Calcutta,
    Pope John XXIII, and Catherine de Hueck Doherty.

CHAPTER TEN

Easter

Easter is the greatest feast of the church year.
It celebrates the rising of Jesus Christ from the dead
     and is often referred to as the "feast of the Resurrection."
Easter is a springtime feast, one associated with new life.
Green grass, budding trees, blooming forsythia, daffodils,
     tulips, dogwood trees, and cherry blossoms
          are all part of Eastertime.
New clothes and Easter bonnets add color and joy
     to what is referred to as "putting on new life."

Easter Eggs

Yosef's Gift of Many Colors, by Cassandre Maxwell,
     is an Easter story set in the Ukraine
     in which the custom and craft of decorating *pysanky*
          is featured.
It is a near perfect story of decorating an Easter egg.
We have discovered that today many children don't experience
     the coloring of eggs in their families,
     so we often do it with them
          during the last class before Easter.

While the children are coloring the eggs,
   we read stories like the one named above,
      or *Rechenka's Eggs*, by Patricia Polacco.
You can find out more about customs surrounding Easter eggs
   in *Catholic Customs & Traditions*, by Greg Dues.

Other Easter Symbols

Other symbols that are part of Easter
are the Paschal candle, Easter fire,
   Easter rabbit, Easter basket,
   and water blessed during the Easter Vigil
      and used throughout the season.
For information about Easter bunnies and baskets, see
   the *Catholic Source Book*, by Peter Klein,
   Advent and Lent Activities for Children,
      by Shiela Kielly and Sheila Geraghty,
   and *Lilies, Rabbits, and Painted Eggs*, by Edna Barth.
The Easter season is a good time to acquaint
   children and young people with these symbols,
      especially the Paschal candle.
They see this symbol in the sanctuary area of the church
   during the fifty days following Easter
      and throughout the rest of the liturgical year.
New fire is used to light the Paschal candle
   during the Easter Vigil on Holy Saturday.
It is an important symbol
   because the light from the new fire
      banishes the darkness associated with Lent
   and is another stirring sign that Christ
      is risen and is with us here and now.
There is no better way to introduce children to the significance
   of the Easter fire than with story,
      especially *Stepka and the Magic Fire*, by Dorothy VanWoerkom.

Resurrection and New Life

In celebrating the feast and the season of Easter,
   we are not only celebrating the rising of Jesus to new life,
     but also resurrection in our own lives.
Children become familiar with this reality in their lives
   as they recover from situations like the separation
   and divorce of parents; the death of a grandparent, parent,
   or friend; the death of a pet; the death of a friendship;
   recovery from an illness; forgiveness and
     healing in relationships.
Themes of resurrection and new life abound in stories,
   although at first glance we might not see them as such.
Since Dad Left, by Caroline Binch, is about a young boy
   who struggles to forgive his Dad after his parents
     don't live together anymore.
In *One April Morning*, by Nancy Lamb,
   fifty Oklahoma City children talk about
   the April 1995 explosion of the Federal Building
     in Oklahoma City and its aftermath.
They share their initial shock and fear,
   their subsequent feelings of guilt and anger,
   and ultimately their sense of hope and healing.
In *The Whispering Cloth*, by Peggy Dietz Shea,
   a child gradually stitches a pa'ndau,
     an embroidered story cloth.
It helps her relive and own her whole story as a refugee,
   the loss of her parents, her rescue by her grandmother,
     and her new life.
In the story *Allison*, by Allen Say, a child discovers
   that she is adopted; this hurts and angers her.
Finally, with the help of a stray cat she befriends,
   she accepts her adoption and her family.

CHAPTER ELEVEN

Jesus, the Center of Our Lives

We revere and honor Jesus because he is central
   to our lives as Christians.
We would like children to own Jesus in their lives.
Jesus is a person totally unto himself,
   but he is also present
      in people who act in a loving way.
It is not only Jesus who is both human and divine.
Each of us is, too, in a way,
   and stories can help us
      enter into the heart of that mystery.

Seeing the Divine in Jesus and in Us

The stories Jesus told clearly show what a person
   looks like when they act in a holy way.
One of these stories is about a poor widow (Luke 21:1–4).
Jesus told many other stories that show what people
   look like when God's life is active in them:
      for example, the parable of the lost sheep.

Another of Jesus' stories is the parable
of the prodigal and his brother,
also known as the prodigal son (Luke 15:11–32).
This story is all about total and unconditional forgiveness.
Jesus told it to show how totally forgiving God is,
and to present a picture of what someone looks like
who forgives.
Jesus not only shows us how to be like God
by the stories he told.
He also models it in his behavior.
One of our favorite stories is about Jesus and Zacchaeus,
the tax collector (Luke 19:1–10).
After a group of third graders heard this story and dramatized it,
one of the girls said this about Jesus, with surprise:
"He was never too good for anyone. He cared about everybody."
The most enduring truth that the Scriptures record about Jesus
is that he cared.
He cared about his mother, his family,
and the guests at a wedding feast (John 2).
He cared about his disciples (John 15),
and friends like Mary Magdalene (John 20),
Mary, Martha, and Lazarus (John 12).
He cared about the sick (Matthew 8, 9; Mark 1, 2; Luke 5),
the hungry (Matthew 14; Mark 6; Luke 9; John 6),
the fearful (Matthew 8:23–27; Mark 4; Luke 8),
sinners (Luke 7:36–50),
and children (Matthew 19:13; Mark 9:36; Luke 9:46).

Children's Bibles and Other Stories

Bringing children together with the story of Jesus
is especially easy today because of the many excellent
Bible story books that have been published.

The Children's Illustrated Bible, by Selena Hastings.

My First Bible, by Ettorina Ottaviani

The Beginner's Bible, by Karyn Henley.

Children of Color Storybook Bible, by Victor Hogan.

The Bible: A People Listen to God, by Joan Baro i Cerqueda.

Tomie de Paola's Book of Bible Stories.

The Parables of Jesus, by Tomie de Paola.

My Bible Friends Read-and-Do Book, by Robin Currie

My Favorite Gospel Activity Book, by Jenny Erickson

My Favorite Bible Activity Book, by Jenny Erickson

The Rhyme Bible, by L. J. Sattgast.

Bible for Young Catholics, by Anne Eileen Heffernan, fsp.

The story of Jesus is also in the story of people, and children's literature is a rich resource of these stories.

Twenty and Ten, by Claire Huchet Bishop. Twenty French children, with the help of a nun, courageously hide and protect ten Jewish children.

The Wednesday Surprise, by Eve Bunting. A little girl lovingly teaches her grandmother to read as a birthday surprise for her father.

The Legend of the Bluebonnet, by Tomie de Paola. A little Indian girl gives up her most prized possession so that rain will fall and save her people.

Brothers, by Florence B. Freedman. Two brothers secretly sacrifice for each other.

Grandmother Bryant's Pocket, by Jacqueline Briggs Martin. A child gradually heals because of the constant and loving care of her grandparents.

Island of the Blue Dolphin, by Scott O'Dell. A child heroically stays behind on an island so her brother will not be alone.

Bibliography

Archambault, Martin and John. *Knots on a Counting Rope.*

Bang, Molly. *The Paper Crane.*

Barth, Edna. *Lilies, Rabbits, and Painted Eggs: The Story of the Easter Symbols.*

Bennett, William J., ed. *The Book of Virtues: A Treasury of Great Moral Stories.*

———. *The Book of Virtues for Young People.*

———. *The Children's Book of Heroes.*

———. *The Children's Book of Virtues.*

Binch, Caroline. *Since Dad Left.*

Bishop, Claire Huchet. *Twenty and Ten.*

Boddy, Marlys. *The Dancing Man.*

———. *The Glassmakers of Gurven.*

Brown, Marcia. *Stone Soup.*

Brown, Margaret Wise. *The Runaway Bunny.*

Brumbeau, Jeff. *The Quiltmaker's Gift.*

Bucholz, Quint. *The Collector of Moments.*

Bunting, Eve. *The Wednesday Surprise.*

Burns, Paul. *Butler's Lives of the Saints,* new full edition.

Canfield, Jack and Mark Victor Hansen. *Chicken Soup for the Soul.*

Cerqueda, Joan Baro. *The Bible: A People Listen to God.*

Clifton, Lucille. *Everett Anderson's Christmas Coming.*

Coles, Robert. *The Story of Ruby Bridges.*

Costello, Gwen. *Praying the Stations with Children.*

Currie, Robin. *My Bible Friends Read-and-Do Book.*

De Paola, Tomie. *The Baby Sister.*

———. *The Legend of the Bluebonnet.*

————. *The Legend of the Persian Carpet.*

————. *The Parables of Jesus.*

————. *The Night of Las Posadas.*

————. *Tomie de Paola's Book of Bible Stories.*

Demi. *The Empty Pot.*

Dues, Greg. *Catholic Customs & Traditions.*

Ellsberg, Robert. *All Saints.*

Erickson, Jenny. *My Favorite Bible Activity Book.*

————. *My Favorite Gospel Activity Book.*

Fleming, Virginia M. *Be Good to Eddie Lee.*

Fox, Mem. *With Love at Christmas.*

Frasier, Debra. *On the Day You Were Born.*

Freedman, Florence B. *Brothers.*

Hastings, Selina. *The Children's Illustrated Bible.*

Hazen, Barbara Shook. *Even If I Did Something Awful?*

Heffernan, Eileen. *Bible for Young Catholics.*

Henry, O. *The Gift of the Magi.*

Henley, Karyn. *The Beginner's Bible: Timeless Children's Stories.*

Hesse, Karen. *Out of the Dust.*

Hickman, Martha Whitmore. *When Can Daddy Come Home?*

Hill, Dave. *The Boy Who Gave His Lunch Away.*

Hoban, Russell. *A Bargain for Frances.*

Hoberman, Mary Ann. *And to Think that We Thought that We'd Never Be Friends.*

Hoffman, Mary. *Amazing Grace.*

Hogan, Victor, illustrator. *Children of Color Storybook Bible.*

Ikeda, Daisaku. *The Cherry Tree.*

Kenneally, Christy. *Miracles and Me.*

————. *Strings and Things.*

Kielly, Shiela and Sheila Geraghty. *Advent and Lent Activities for Children: Camels, Carols, Crosses, and Crowns.*

Klein, Lee. *The Best Gift for Mom.*

Klein, Peter. *The Catholic Source Book.*

Kramer, Janice. *Eight Bags of Gold.*

Lamb, Nancy. *One April Morning.*

Lionni, Leo. *Little Blue and Little Yellow.*

————. *Swimmy.*

————. *Tico and the Golden Wings.*

Lucado, Max. *Jacob's Gift.*

Martin, Jacqueline Briggs. *Grandmother Bryant's Pocket.*

Mathis, Sharon Bell. *The Hundred Penny Box.*

Maxwell, Cassandre. *Yosef's Gift of Many Colors.*

Mayer, Mercer. *Shibumi and the Kitemaker.*

McCourt, Lisa. *The Braids Girl* (*Chicken Soup for Little Souls* series).

Mills, Lauren. *The Rag Coat.*

Munsch, Robert. *Love You Forever.*

Naylor, Phyllis Reynolds. *Shiloh.*

Neuberger, Anne E. *Advent Stories and Activities: Meeting Jesus through the Jesse Tree.*

O'Dell, Scott. *Island of the Blue Dolphins.*

Ottaviani, Ettorina. *My First Bible.*

Polacco, Patricia. *Mrs. Katz and Tush.*

————. *Rechenka's Eggs.*

————. *The Trees of the Dancing Goats.*

Porter, Daniel J. *Shalinar's Song.*

Raschka, Christopher. *Yo! Yes?.*

Rollins, Charlamae Hill, ed. *Christmas Gif': An Anthology of Christmas Poems, Songs, and Stories Written By and About African Americans.*

Rylant, Cynthia. *An Angel for Solomon Singer.*

Sabuda, Robert. *Saint Valentine*.

Sasso, Sandy Eisenberg. *In God's Name*.

Sattgast, L.J. *The Rhyme Bible*.

Say, Allen. *Allison*.

Shea, Peggy Dietz. *The Whispering Cloth*.

Shepard, Aaron. *The Crystal Heart: A Vietnamese Legend*.

Silverstein, Shel. *Where the Sidewalk Ends*.

Speare, Elizabeth George. *The Witch of Blackbeard Pond*.

Spier, Peter. *People*.

Steptoe, John. *The Story of Jumping Mouse: A Native American Legend*.

Taylor, Theodore. *Maria*.

———. *The Cay*.

Tolstoy, Leo. *Shoemaker Martin*.

VanWoerkom, Dorothy. *Stepka and the Magic Fire*.

Wakefield, Charito Calvachi. *Navidad latinoamericana/ Latin American Christmas*.

Wild, Margaret. *Let the celebrations begin!*

Wilde, Oscar. *The Selfish Giant*.

Wildsmith, Brian. *A Christmas Story*.

Wilkeshuis, Cornelia. *The Best Gift of All*.

Wojciechowski, Susan. *The Christmas Miracle of Jonathan Toomey*.

Yacowitz, Caryn. *The Jade Stone*.